Sheffield Hallam University
Learning and IT Services
Adsetts Centre City Campus
Sheffield   S1 1WB

D1632975

Developing Science

DEVELOPING SCIENTIFIC SKILLS AND KNOWLEDGE

year

SHEFFIELD HALLAM UNIVERSITY
LEARNING CENTRE
WITHDRAWN FROM STOCK

Christine Moorcroft

A & C BLACK

Contents

SHEFFIELD HALLAM UNIVERSITY
WL
TP 500
MO
COLLEGIATE CRESCENT
Teaching Practice

Rocks and soils

Magnets and springs

Light and shadows

Published 2004 by A & C Black Publishers Limited
37 Soho Square, London W1D 3QZ
www.acblack.com

ISBN 0-7136-6642-0

Copyright text © Christine Moorcroft, 2004
Copyright illustrations © Kirsty Wilson, 2004
Copyright cover illustration © Kay Widdowson, 2004
Editor: Jane Klima
Design: Susan McIntyre

The author and publishers would like to thank Catherine Yemm,
Trevor Davies and the staff of Balsall Common Primary School
for their assistance in producing this series of books.

A CIP catalogue record for this book is available from the
British Library.

All rights reserved. This book may be photocopied, for use in
the school or educational establishment for which it was
purchased, but may not be reproduced in any other form or
by any other means – graphic, electronic or mechanical,
including recording, taping or information retrieval systems –
without the prior permission in writing of the publishers.

Printed in Great Britain by St Edmundsbury Press Ltd,
Bury St Edmunds, Suffolk.

A & C Black uses paper produced with elemental chlorine-free
pulp, harvested from managed sustainable forests.

Introduction

Developing Science is a series of seven photocopiable activity books for science lessons. Each book provides a range of activities that not only develop children's knowledge and understanding of science, but also offer opportunities to develop their scientific skills: planning experimental work and obtaining and considering evidence.

The activities vary in their approach: some are based on first-hand observations, some present the findings of investigations for the children to analyse and others require the children to find information from books and electronic sources. They focus on different parts of a scientific investigation: questioning, responding to questions, generating ideas, planning, predicting, carrying out a fair test or an investigation, recording findings, checking and questioning findings, explaining findings and presenting explanations.

The activities in **Year 3** are based on Science in the National Curriculum and the QCA scheme of work for Year 3. They provide opportunities for the children to:

- develop curiosity about the things they observe and experience, and explore the world with all their senses;
- use this experience to develop their understanding of key scientific ideas and make links between different phenomena and experiences;
- begin to think about models to represent things they cannot directly experience;
- try to make sense of phenomena, seeking explanations and thinking critically about claims and ideas;
- acquire and refine the practical skills needed to investigate questions safely;
- develop skills of predicting, asking questions, making inferences, concluding and evaluating (based on evidence and understanding), and use these skills in investigative work;
- practise mathematical skills such as counting, ordering numbers, measuring using standard and non-standard measures and recording and interpreting simple charts;
- learn why numerical and mathematical skills are useful and helpful to understanding;
- think creatively about science and enjoy trying to make sense of phenomena;
- develop language skills through talking about their work and presenting their own ideas, using systematic writing of different kinds;
- use scientific and mathematical language (including technical vocabulary and conventions) and draw pictures, diagrams and charts to communicate scientific ideas;
- read non-fiction and extract information from sources such as reference books or CD-ROMs;
- work with others, listening to their ideas and treating these with respect;
- develop respect for evidence and evaluate critically ideas which may or may not fit the evidence available;
- develop a respect for the environment and living things and for their own health and safety.

The activities are carefully linked with the National Literacy Strategy to give the children opportunities to develop their reading skills in finding information (for example, scanning a text, reading instructions and making notes) and to use a range of writing skills in presenting their findings (for example, labelling diagrams and writing simple reports). Science-related vocabulary to introduce is provided in the **Notes on the activities** on pages 5–11.

Teachers are encouraged to introduce the activities presented in this book in a stimulating classroom environment that provides facilities for the children to explore, through play, using movement and the senses. For example, you could provide an activity corner where the children can investigate materials, equipment, pictures and books connected with the topics to be covered (such as magnets and rocks), or you could use role play or PE lessons to explore movements (such as the ways springs behave).

Each activity sheet specifies the learning outcome and has a **Teachers' note** at the foot of the page, which you may wish to mask before photocopying. Expanded teaching notes are provided in the **Notes on the activities**. Most activities also end with a challenge (**Now try this!**), which reinforces the children's learning and provides the teacher with an opportunity for assessment. These activities might be appropriate for only a few children; it is not expected that the whole class should complete them. The extension activities should be completed in a notebook or on a separate sheet of paper.

Health and safety

Developing Science recognises the importance of safety in science lessons and provides advice on the ways in which teachers can make their lessons as safe as possible (including links to useful websites). The books also suggest ways in which to encourage children to take appropriate responsibility for their own safety. Teachers are recommended to follow the safety guidelines provided in the QCA scheme of work or in *Be Safe!* (available from the Association for Science Education). Specific health and safety advice is included in the **Notes on the activities** and warnings to the children feature on the activity sheets where relevant.

Online resources

In addition to the photocopiable activity sheets in this book, a collection of online science resources is available on the A & C Black website at www.acblack.com/developingscience. These activities can be used either as stand-alone teaching resources or in conjunction with the printed sheets. An ICT icon on an activity page indicates that there is a resource on the website specifically designed to complement that activity.

To enable them to be used by children of a wide range of abilities, all the activities on the website feature both written and spoken instructions. The tasks have been designed to provide experiences that are not easy to reproduce in the classroom: for example, children can take a virtual tour of a street to look for materials or see how manufacturers test fabrics.

Notes on the activities

These notes expand upon those provided at the foot of the activity pages. They give ideas for making the most of the activity sheet, including suggestions for the whole-class introduction, the plenary session or for follow-up work using an adapted version of the activity sheet. To help teachers to select appropriate learning experiences for their pupils, the activities are grouped into sections within each book, but the pages need not be presented in the order in which they appear, unless stated otherwise. Where appropriate, links to other areas of the curriculum are indicated, in particular to literacy and numeracy.

Teeth and eating

Shopping basket: 1 and **2** (pages 12–13) focus on the different kinds of food we eat. You could show the children pictures of foods from each group and discuss the meanings of any new words. If possible, let the children sort a real bag of shopping onto labelled shelves (using empty packets where necessary). You could make a connection with literacy by focusing on names of foods that are compound words.

Vocabulary: *dairy, diet, drink, fats, fish, food, fruit, meat, nuts, pulses, seeds, starches, sugars, variety, vegetables, water.*

Fit to eat (page 14) is about the purposes for which our bodies use different types of food. The children might know that some athletes, such as long-distance runners, eat pasta the evening before their event. Discuss why. What other foods do athletes eat for energy? Point out that all foods help us to be active but that our bodies can make use of some more quickly than others. Tell the children that our bodies are made from materials from foods, but that some foods provide more of these useful materials than others. You could also discuss the types of foods that are missing from this page that help us to stay healthy, such as fruits and vegetables and water. Link this to literacy by focusing on phonemes in the names of foods.

Vocabulary: *active, energy, feed, growth.*

Food for thought (page 15) looks at the variety of foods we eat and how some diets differ from others: for example, slimming diets, diets based on regional or ethnic foods, vegetarian and vegan diets, diets based on religious or other beliefs and diets followed for health reasons such as an allergy to nuts or flour. Discuss the ways in which menus and food labels can help with special diets. Link this with non-fiction writing in literacy lessons.

Vocabulary: *diet, choice, health, menu, religious, slimming, vegan, vegetarian.*

Dog's dinner (page 16) helps the children to explore the foods that dogs eat and to record their findings. It can be linked with data handling in mathematics. Encourage the children to discuss what they have found out. For the extension activity, the children might suggest conducting a survey of friends with dogs to find out whether their dog gets the chance to eat what it likes best. The survey should ask who chooses what their dog eats. Can the dog choose? Does it get the opportunity to hunt for its own food? How can it show whether it likes the food it is given or not? Point out that most dogs eat food chosen by their owners, although if they do not like a food they will not eat it.

Vocabulary: *choice, feed, like, prefer.*

Food watch (page 17) encourages the children to predict what a snail will eat, plan a fair test and record their findings. It provides an opportunity to focus on different ways of recording

 Salt harms (and usually kills) snails. The children should keep their hands away from their faces during this investigation and wash their hands afterwards.

information. The children might suggest putting each food on a large sheet of paper at an equal distance from the snail so that it has the same chance to find each of them. They might also suggest returning the snail to the centre of the paper after it has tried each food and turning it to face a different direction. Another consideration is that the snail might not be hungry after it has eaten one or two foods, so it does not eat the others even if it likes them. Ask the children how they can find out if it likes the other foods. Also ask them if they think all snails like the same foods and, if so, how they can find out.

Vocabulary: *choice, fair test, findings, prefer, record.*

Our teeth (page 18) introduces the terms *milk teeth* and *second teeth* or *adult teeth* and encourages the children to make and record observations of their own teeth. Explain that second teeth or adult teeth replace the milk teeth, but that no more teeth will grow to replace them. Point out that the diagram shows a full set of adult teeth and that few of the children, if any, will have all these teeth. This page offers a useful connection with numeracy (recording data on a table).

Vocabulary: *adult teeth, milk teeth, second teeth.*

A bite to eat (page 19) concerns the purposes and names of the different types of teeth we have and how we use them. The children could talk about the ways in which they use

 Use only replica teeth or those that have been sterilised thoroughly.

their teeth to eat different foods: for example, bread, chocolate, an orange, thick soup, toffee. You could also show them samples of extracted teeth of different types so that they can see the parts usually hidden inside the gums. You could link this activity with literacy work on writing descriptions using adjectives.

Vocabulary: *bite, canine, chew, cut, incisor, molar, tear.*

A toothy tale (page 20) is about the differences between milk teeth and adult teeth and encourages the children to consider why adult teeth should be cared for especially well. The children could talk about the experiences they and others in their families have had of fillings and extractions. They could also use these experiences to write a recount in a literacy lesson.

Vocabulary: *adult tooth, extraction, filling, milk tooth, toothache.*

A healthy smile (page 21) develops the children's understanding of how we can keep our teeth and gums healthy. It is useful if they have first completed pages 12–14. You could help them to make displays about dental care and about the foods that help to build healthy teeth and exercise the gums. Foods containing the materials from which teeth are formed include dairy foods, green vegetables and pulses; foods that help to maintain healthy gums include apples, avocados, carrots, dairy foods, fish, meat and nuts. Provide leaflets from doctors' surgeries, health centres, supermarkets and chemists giving information about foods. This offers a useful link with literacy (reading non-fiction texts for information). It is important not to brand any foods as bad in case the children are given them at home. But point out that certain foods (sugary foods and acidic foods such as citrus fruits) are more likely than others to form acids in the mouth that can damage the teeth. We need not stop eating these foods but should avoid eating them over long periods (with a meal is best) and should rinse out the mouth or brush the teeth after a meal and before going to bed.

Vocabulary: *gums, healthy, rinse, toothbrush, toothpaste.*

Helping plants grow well

 Harvest time (page 22) broadens the children's knowledge of food plants. Provide leaflets and information books about food plants so that the children can use secondary sources to check their ideas. This develops literacy skills in researching information. Children who undertake the extension activity could include in their report how the plant is processed before it is used as a food. A complementary activity for this sheet is available on the website (see Year 3 Activity 1).

School and LEA guidelines should be followed for any visits.

Vocabulary: *allotment, greengrocery, market garden.*

The leaf thief (page 23) helps the children to understand that a plant needs leaves in order to grow and to survive, but that it can manage if it loses some of them. The children might mention plants that survive without leaves (for example, trees and bushes in winter and dormant bulbs and rhizomes). You can explain how these are different from seedlings and small potted plants after the children have carried out their investigation. Some plants look as if they are dead in the winter; they are not dead, but dormant, and so do not need food. Plants that grow from bulbs and rhizomes have dormant periods. Explain that dormant plants are similar to hibernating animals. Provide five plants of the same type and about the same size (geraniums are suitable). One should be grown as a control (with none of its leaves removed) and one should have all its leaves cut off. Help the children to count half of another plant's leaves, about a quarter of another's leaves and about three-quarters of another's leaves, and to cut them off. Label the plants. This is a useful opportunity to develop numeracy skills in simple fractions. The children should realise that all the plants should be treated in the same way except for the number of leaves removed: kept in the same place, in the same kind of pot and soil, and given the same amount of water.

Vocabulary: *growth, leaves, observe.*

Rooted to the spot (page 24) provides a ready-made chart on which the children can record their measurements of the growth of plants in different-sized pots to find out whether plants grow better when they have more space for their roots. Discuss what difference a larger pot makes to the roots of a plant and how this might affect its growth. Provide one plant that has outgrown its pot and another plant of the same type in a suitably sized pot. The children should measure the height of each plant from the base of the stem to its tip. Discuss what else they can record apart from the height: for example, the size and number of leaves and any flowers. This provides useful practice in the numeracy skills of handling data and measuring in standard units. Discuss what the roots of a plant are for (to anchor it in the ground and to take in water and minerals) and why a re-potted plant should grow better (the roots can spread out and take in more water).

Vocabulary: *bigger, roots, size, stronger.*

In **Sucking it up** (page 25) the children learn that the water taken in by a plant's roots is drawn up through the stem to other parts of the plant by observing the water rising up a celery stem. Recording their observations at fixed intervals gives the children practice in numeracy skills associated with time. The celery should be placed in shallow water coloured with food dye or ink, so that it shows through the stem. You could also show the children what happens when a narrow drinking straw is left to stand in a pot of coloured water (the water rises up the straw). Draw attention to the holes in the stem of the celery and ask how these are like straws (they are narrow tubes, up which water will rise).

Resources: a head of celery ● a transparent pot ● food colouring or ink ● magnifying glasses ● a timer

Vocabulary: *celery, colour, dye, rise, suck, tube, water.*

Enough water: 1, 2 and **3** (pages 26–28) develop the children's understanding that plants grow better the more water they have, up to a certain amount, after which they become waterlogged and do not grow well. These three pages help the children to turn a question into a form that can be investigated, to record the growth of seedlings on a ready-made bar chart and then to evaluate their investigation and to suggest improvements. They also develop numeracy skills in handling data and measuring in standard units. The children should compare four seedlings each given a fixed amount of water (or, in one case, none at all) each day. Suggest the amounts of water: 'a small amount' (5 cm³), 'a medium amount' (20 cm³) and 'a lot' (50 cm³). To simplify this activity, the children could measure the water in teaspoonfuls (1 teaspoonful is about 5 ml): 1 tsp, 4 tsp, 10 tsp. The seedlings should be grown in the same conditions of light and warmth and the same kind of pots or trays and growing medium. Page 27 provides space for notes: for example, the condition and colour of the stem and leaves (*green, stringy, strong, thin, yellow*).

Resources: four plant seedlings of the same type (for example, beans, marigolds or cress), in the same type of pot and growing medium ● a ruler

Vocabulary: *growth, healthiest, healthy, height, investigation, observe, record, seedling, strength, unhealthiest, unhealthy, waterlogged.*

For **In the dark: 1** and **2** (pages 29–30) the children evaluate an investigation into how a lack of sunlight affects the growth of grass, suggest improvements and then plan another investigation (about what happens to other plants). The children might think that the bricks will stop the grass growing because they are heavy. Discuss what might stop plants growing. Establish that the test is fairer if a bucket is used because this will prove that it is the lack of light and not the weight of the bricks that stops the grass growing healthily. This activity could also be used to complement literacy work on opposites (*light/dark, light/heavy, healthy/unhealthy*).

> **Resources:** a patch of short grass ● bucket
> ● a collection of plants or seedlings of the same type
> ● a means of covering the plants to keep out light ● rulers

> **Vocabulary:** *fair, growth, investigation, measure, observe, unfair.*

Hothouse plants (page 31) develops the children's understanding of fair and unfair testing. They are asked to evaluate a suggested (unfair) investigation and to suggest improvements: the plants are not given the same amounts of light, they are planted in different containers and in different growing mediums and different types and sizes of plants are compared. Only the temperature should be different for each plant. The children could carry out the investigations they suggest during subsequent lessons. You could also link this activity with literacy lessons on writing instructions.

> **Vocabulary:** *fair, measure, observe, warmth, unfair.*

Characteristics of materials

ICT **Material world** (page 32) revises previous learning about the different types of materials used for making everyday things. It develops the children's understanding of what makes some materials better than others for particular purposes. Help them to decide which materials come into the categories of 'fabric', 'metal', 'stone' and so on: for example, concrete and tiles can be classed as 'stone'. This discussion also extends the children's vocabulary. A complementary activity for this sheet is available on the website (see Year 3 Activity 2).

> **Vocabulary:** *concrete, fabric, frame, glass, handle, material, metal, object, pane, socket, stone, suitable, wood.*

A closer look (page 33) encourages the children to consider the properties of particular materials and what makes those materials suitable for making particular objects: for example, Children should not handle glass objects in school. ceramics, glass, metal and plastic. Provide collections of objects of the same type but made of different materials: for example, combs made of plastic and metal; spoons made of metal, plastic and wood; rulers made of wood and plastic. Focus on the relevant qualities such as strength, toughness, transparency, hardness, flexibility. As a literacy exercise, encourage the use of as many adjectives as possible to describe the different materials.

> **Vocabulary:** *breakable, ceramics, flexible, glass, hard, hardwearing, metal, opaque, plastic, strong, tough, transparent, wood.*

Guess which material? (page 34) develops the children's ability to recognise the qualities of materials: flexibility, hardness, strength, toughness and so on. Some children could carry out this activity orally, with an adult helper, describing samples of materials hidden from view. Their descriptions could be written up and displayed along with the samples.

> **Resources:** everyday objects made of different
> materials: ceramics, fabrics, metal, plastic, wood

> **Vocabulary:** *bendy, break, breakable, crumple, flexible, fold, fragile, hard, opaque, soft, strong, translucent, transparent.*

Splat test (page 35) builds skills in planning an investigation and in recognising fair and unfair tests. It also develops the children's ability to measure and record their findings. They should ensure that they use the same ball of Plasticine to test each surface (rolling it back into a ball after each test); they should drop it from the same height each time, and not throw it. They should draw round the 'splat' (the flattened side of the ball of Plasticine) and count the squares it covers. The more squares covered the bigger the splat and therefore the harder the surface. To make the test fair, the surfaces should as far as possible be equally elastic. A Plasticine ball dropped onto a fairly hard, springy surface such as a trampoline might not have as great a 'splat' as one dropped onto a softer but less elastic material. Ask the children to look at their recorded results and to say which is the biggest splat and what this tells them about the hardness of the surfaces. You could relate this activity to measuring area in numeracy.

> **Resources:** balls of Plasticine ● different floor
> surfaces ● a long ruler or tape measure

> **Vocabulary:** *area, fair, hard, hardness, height, measure, squares, unfair.*

ICT **Tough stuff** (page 36) allows the children to test their scientific ideas by planning a test and deciding if it is fair. They could time how long they rub each material or they could count the rubs (each rub would have to be the same length – the children could chalk two marks on the ground about 50 cm apart and rub the fabric over this distance). They also need to try to rub each material equally hard. Discuss how they will know which materials are hardwearing. This page could be used in conjunction with a literacy exercise on writing reports. Ask the children to write a report about one of the fabrics. A complementary activity for this sheet is available on the website (see Year 3 Activity 3).

> **Resources:** samples of fabric: cotton, denim, nylon, silk,
> wool ● a large stone or half a brick ● a rough surface
> (for example, concrete or paving stones) ● a ruler
> ● (possibly) a timer or stopwatch

> **Vocabulary:** *cotton, denim, fabric, hardwearing, measure, nylon, silk, tough, wool.*

In **Soak it up: 1** and **2** (pages 37–38) the children plan and carry out a fair test of the absorbency of papers, deciding what evidence to collect and to record and interpreting their results. Draw attention to the textures and surfaces of materials they know are absorbent, such as towelling and sponge: they have holes in them. Remind them of how water is taken up the stems of plants (page 25) and the ways in which these materials are similar to the stem of the celery (they have holes which can soak up water). You will need to help the children to decide what is the best size of paper to test; a piece that is too small will not soak up even 5 ml of water whereas a piece that is too big will soak up more than 30 ml. The graph format helps the children to record their findings. Look at the graphs during the plenary session: ask which paper absorbed most water and how they can tell from the graph. This makes a useful link with numeracy skills in handling data, interpreting data and measuring volume in standard units.

Resources: samples of papers (for example, kitchen roll, tissue paper, shiny paper, sugar paper, blotting paper and writing paper) ● scissors ● small measuring containers (the type supplied for measuring doses of medicine is useful) ● a dropper

Vocabulary: *absorb, absorbent, compare, improve, measure, millilitre, sample, soak, water.*

ICT Full stretch (page 39) focuses on how the properties of materials make them suitable for particular purposes, and develops the children's skills in evaluating tests. The children could carry out some 'dummy runs' of investigations to decide what they need to keep the same for each pair of tights tested. Draw their attention to the need to measure each pair of tights *before* it is stretched as well as during stretching, and to determine the amount of stretch (since some might be longer than others to begin with). Discuss how the children will be able to tell which are the stretchiest tights. Ask if the longest tights stretched the most. Some children might need help in identifying the factors that make the test fair. Suggest ensuring that each pair of tights is stretched the same amount (a ruler could be used to measure the stretch or a non-standard measure could be used: for example, a length of wood, or the same number of stones could be put into the feet of each pair of tights). Encourage the children to identify any potential hazards and to devise safety rules for the investigation. You could relate this sheet to a lesson on organising information and writing instructions in literacy. A complementary activity for this sheet is available on the website (see Year 3 Activity 4).

Resources: several pairs of tights of different types ● weights ● a ruler

Vocabulary: *elastic, elasticity, fair, material, measure, stretch, stretchy, stretchiest, unfair.*

Suit yourself (page 40) looks at the qualities which make some materials suitable for making particular objects, and develops the children's ability to identify those properties. Elasticity tests could be similar to those suggested for tights (page 39). Test how opaque the materials are when wet by holding them in front of lights of varying brightness (beginning with a dim light shining through layers of paper, removing a layer at a time to see if the wet material is still opaque when a bright light is shone on it and then recording the number of layers of paper – the fewest means the brightest light and therefore the most opaque material). How quick-drying the materials are could be tested by soaking them in the same amount of water, rolling them in a towel to remove the excess and hanging them in the

same place to dry. The children should feel them after agreed intervals and record how long they take to dry. Encourage the children to identify any potential hazards and to devise safety rules for the investigation. Some children will need support in planning an investigation. It is helpful to suggest 'silly' ideas for materials: for example, 'Would a fur swimsuit be a good idea? … Why not?' or 'Should a swimsuit be made of transparent material? … Why not?' The instructions exercise on this sheet could be completed in a literacy lesson, focusing on the use of the imperative form of verbs.

Resources: samples of fabrics ● other materials will vary according to what the children decide to test, but it is useful to have the following to hand: timers ● a strong torch ● pieces of paper of the same type ● weights ● rulers

Vocabulary: *absorbent, describe, elastic, fabric, hardwearing, material, opaque, quality, quick-drying, stretchy, strong, translucent, transparent, washable, waterproof.*

Rocks and soils

ICT All kinds of rocks (page 41) encourages the children to make careful observations of rocks. You could introduce the names of different types of rock, but it is not necessary for the children to learn them all at this stage. It is also useful to show the children pictures of various landscapes and talk about the rocks showing on the surface and those that cannot be seen. Samples of common rocks can be purchased from educational suppliers or from museums. *Usborne Spotter's Guide: Rocks and Minerals* (Usborne) is a very useful and simple guide. See also:
www.bbc.co.uk/education/rocks/
http://dph1701.tripod.com/geology/
www.geolab.unc.edu/Petunia/IgMetAtlas/mainmenu.html
http://volcano.und.nodak.edu/vwdocs/vwlessons/lessons/Slideshow/Slideindex.html
www.learn.co.uk/glearning/primary/lessons/ks2/rocks3/default.asp
In a literacy lesson, you could ask the children to make a glossary about rocks. A complementary activity for this sheet is available on the website (see Year 3 Activity 5).

Resources: rock samples (chalk, granite, limestone, pumice, quartz, sandstone, slate) ● magnifying glasses

Vocabulary: *dull, flat, holes, matt, ridge, rough, sharp, shiny, smooth, speckled, surface, texture, white.*

Hard as rock (page 42) helps the children to understand how the hardness of rocks can be tested. They might find a rock that cannot be scratched by the implements they try. If so, encourage them to suggest something harder with which they could try to scratch it: for example, a woodworking file. Encourage the children to suggest rules for using tools safely. They could do this in a literacy lesson focusing on writing instructions.

Resources: rock samples (chalk, granite, limestone, pumice, quartz, sandstone, slate) ● a nail-file ● a 2p coin, ● a nail (about 5 cm long)

Vocabulary: *compare, hardness, measure, record, scratch.*

Passing through (page 43) helps the children to plan and carry out a test to find out how well water soaks into or through rocks. You could introduce words such as *permeable* and *impermeable* and link them with literacy work on opposites and prefixes.

Resources: rock samples (chalk, granite, limestone, pumice, sandstone, slate) ● a dropper ● water

> **Vocabulary:** *impermeable, permeable, soak.*

 Hard facts (page 44) focuses on the qualities of rocks that make them suitable for different purposes. Remind the children of qualities such as hardness, roughness, shine, smoothness, toughness. See also the websites listed under the notes for page 41. The extension activity could be completed in a literacy lesson. Some children could write a simple non-chronological report about one type of rock (for example, where it comes from, how it is treated and how and where it is used); others could research and make notes. A complementary activity for this sheet is available on the website (see Year 3 Activity 6).

> **Vocabulary:** *chalk, granite, hard, limestone, pumice, quartz, rough, sandstone, shiny, smooth, soft, sparkling.*

 In **Bits and pieces** (page 45) the children examine soil samples to learn that they are different depending on where they come from. It

> ⚠ Soil samples should be taken from areas free from cat and dog faeces. The children should wash their hands after handling soil.

is important to point out that there is always rock beneath the soil and that bits of rock wear away and form soil. Soil also has animal and plant remains in it. To help the children to decide if the soils are 'gritty', 'sharp' or 'silky', ask them to compare them with other materials that have been labelled 'gritty', 'sharp' and 'silky': granulated sugar, preserving sugar and flour. If not available locally, soil samples can be bought from TTS, Nunn Brook Road, Huthwaite, Sutton-in-Ashfield NG17 2HU: www.tts-shopping.com. Like many of the activities connected with materials, this sheet provides an opportunity for work on adjectives during literacy lessons. A complementary activity for this sheet and for pages 46–47 is available on the website (see Year 3 Activity 7).

Resources: four samples of soil from different places ● sieves or riddles with holes of different sizes ● magnifying glasses

> **Vocabulary:** *grade, particle, riddle, rock, sample, sieve, soil, wear.*

 Waterlogged: 1 and **2** (pages 46–47) develop the children's skills in recognising and planning a fair test, measuring time, using simple apparatus to measure volume and using their results to make comparisons and draw conclusions. They should notice that Kim and Joe compare different amounts of soil, put them in different-sized containers and measure neither the amount of water poured onto the soil nor the amount that flows through, and they do not time the experiment. Some children could complete the extension activity on page 46 in a literacy lesson. Other children could make a simple list of the problems with the test. In a subsequent science lesson, the children could compare samples of clay and sand by placing the same amount of each in plastic pots with small holes pierced in the base, pouring in a measured amount of water and measuring how much of it has soaked through the soil in a given time (they might have to have a trial run to decide how long). After completing the test, the children should comment on their results. What have they found out about the soils? Did the comparison answer their question? A complementary activity for these sheets and for page 45 is available on the website (see Year 3 Activity 7).

Resources: samples of clay and sand ● plastic pots with small holes in the base ● measuring jugs ● pots in which to catch the water soaking through the soil ● a timer or stopwatch

> **Vocabulary:** *clay, holes, porous, sand, soak.*

Magnets and springs

Poles apart (page 48) helps the children to understand the ways in which magnets can attract and repel one another. They could later investigate magnets whose poles have been marked and describe what happens when two north poles, two south poles or a north and a south pole meet. This complements literacy work on opposites (*north/south, attract/repel, together/apart*). Magnets should be handled with care; dropping or knocking them can weaken them. Keepers – pieces of wood or steel placed between magnets or across their poles – should be used during storage.

Resources: bar magnets ● horseshoe magnets (including strong alnico magnets) ● ring magnets ● rod magnets

> **Vocabulary:** *alnico magnet, attract, bar magnet, force, horseshoe magnet, north, pole, pull, push, repel, ring magnet, rod magnet, south.*

Magnet puzzles (page 49) teaches the children that magnets attract some, but not all, metals; it develops skills in making and testing predictions, making careful observations and using results to draw conclusions. After predicting which mixtures can be separated using a magnet, they can check their predictions using a magnet. (A strong alnico magnet will pick up magnetic recording tape.) Discuss any surprises. They might have thought that all metals would be attracted. Explain that the common metals that are attracted are iron and steel (which is made from iron) and that other metals – nickel and cobalt (used to magnetise recording tape) – are also attracted. Point out that 'tin' cans are made from steel coated with tin to stop it rusting. Aluminium cans (often used as drinks containers) do not have a tin coating because aluminium does not rust. Tell the children the names of the metals; they need not remember them all, except for iron and steel, at this stage.

> **Vocabulary:** *aluminium, attract, force, iron, magnet, metal, pull, push, separate, steel, tin.*

Everyday magnets (page 50) tells the children about the variety of uses magnets have. As a homework activity they could look for other examples at home and during another lesson they could make up a game using magnets. During a literacy lesson they could write instructions for their game.

> **Vocabulary:** *attract, force, iron, magnet, metal, pull, push, steel.*

Strong magnets: 1 and **2** (pages 51–52) encourage the children to investigate an aspect of the behaviour of magnets. They develop the children's skills in planning a fair test and identifying what they should measure. Page 51 provides a starting point, suggests equipment and offers a framework to help the children to plan their test; page 52 focuses on the identification of what is fair and what is unfair. Only the third illustration shows a fair test (just one pole of each magnet has been used, the paper clips are all the same size and are hanging in one line). The other three tests are not comparing like with like: the paper clips are hanging from different parts of the magnets; bunches of paper clips have been picked up in a random way; the paper clips are different sizes. No recording chart is provided, since the children might come up with different things to measure or count (for example, the distance from which a magnet attracts a paper clip or the number of paper clips it will pick up). These pages could be linked with literacy work on connectives (*because, so that, if*).

Resources: four different magnets ● paper clips ● rulers

> **Vocabulary:** *attract, force, magnet, strong, stronger, strongest, weak, weaker, weakest.*

Pulling through (page 53) provides an opportunity to investigate another aspect of the behaviour of magnets and to draw conclusions from observations. The materials tested should be, as far as possible, of the same thickness. Ask the children if they think a magnet will work through stone. If it does not, is this because the stone is too thick? Using a very strong magnet, they could test very thin pieces of stone such as slate. For the extension activity set rules: magnets should not be put into liquids, and must be kept dry. The children could put paper clips into pots containing the liquid and use the magnet on the outside of the pot. Magnets do not work through magnetic materials such as iron and steel.

Resources: strong magnets ● paper clips ● pieces of kitchen foil, cotton, leather, steel (for example, a tea tray), cardboard, wood, plastic and iron) of about the same thickness

> **Vocabulary:** *attract, force, liquid, magnet, predict, prediction, through.*

Springy things (page 54) focuses on the uses of springs in everyday situations. Let the children open a torch or a ballpoint pen to find out 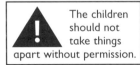 The children should not take things apart without permission. what the spring does. They could put the pen back together without the spring and notice the difference. Discuss what the springs are pushing. Use the word *force* to refer to the push, and draw attention to the directions of the pushes.

Resources: a ballpoint pen ● a torch

> **Vocabulary:** *force, push, spring.*

Spring into action (page 55) develops understanding that when a spring is compressed it exerts a force on whatever is compressing it, and that forces act in particular directions. The children who do the extension activity could put a spring underneath different weights (inside a container such as a clear plastic tube) and observe how much each spring shortens when it is pushed down by the same weight:

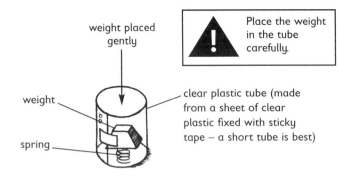

weight placed gently

Place the weight in the tube carefully.

weight

clear plastic tube (made from a sheet of clear plastic fixed with sticky tape – a short tube is best)

spring

Draw attention to the spellings of new words (*compress, exert, force*) and encourage the use of appropriate spelling strategies.

Resources: a collection of springs (from educational suppliers or from broken toys and other equipment)

> **Vocabulary:** *compress, exert, force, push, spring, strong, stronger, strongest, weak, weaker, weakest.*

At a stretch (page 56) develops the children's understanding that when an elastic band is stretched it exerts a force on whatever is stretching it, and that forces act in The children should let go of elastic bands gently after stretching them. particular directions. They could find out what happens after an elastic band has been stretched. Does it go back to the same size as it was before? Does this depend on how much it was stretched (and for how long)? You could link this with numeracy – measuring in small standard units.

Resources: elastic bands of different lengths and thickness

> **Vocabulary:** *elastic, force, pull, stretch.*

Launch pad (page 57) practises skills in making predictions about the effects of stretching elastic bands by different amounts, making comparisons, identifying patterns in results and drawing conclusions from the results. Do the children think that the more the elastic is stretched the further the car will travel? Ask them to suggest some simple safety rules: for example, they could consider the limit to which it is safe to stretch the elastic (this limit could be chalked on the ground). After they have completed the activity, ask them what they have found out from their results. Also ask them about the direction in which they pulled, the direction in which the elastic pulled and the direction in which the car travelled. This page can be linked with measuring in larger standard units (metres).

Resources: dressmaking elastic or a series of elastic bands fastened together in a chain ● a ruler ● a long tape measure ● two chairs ● a robust toy car

> **Vocabulary:** *elastic, force, pull, push, stretch.*

Light and shadows

Before the children begin these activities they need to observe what happens to light from the Sun and artificial light sources when it is blocked by an object. A beam of light continues without stopping (although it loses intensity) unless it is blocked by an opaque object. An opaque object blocking the path of a ray of light will reflect some light and absorb some, depending on the colour and texture of its surface. This need not be explained unless the children ask about it. The activities focus on establishing that a shadow is an absence of light, that light travels in straight lines and that the direction of the light source affects the shape, size and direction of shadows.

Shine a light (page 58) shows that a shadow is a place where there is little or no light, caused when something blocks the path of a beam of light, and that light travels in straight lines. The children should notice that the holes in the cards have to be lined up in order to let the light shine through all four pieces of card and that, if one card is turned so that its hole is out of alignment, a shadow will be cast on the next one.

Resources: a torch ● four pieces of card about 10 cm square ● Plasticine

> **Vocabulary:** *beam, block, darkness, light, shadow, shine, straight, torch.*

Make a shadow (page 59) develops understanding that shadows are formed when light travelling from a source is blocked and that shadows are similar in shape to the objects forming them. Revise previous learning about shadows: that they are made when something blocks the path of a beam of light. The children should notice that the higher they hold the torch the shorter the shadow of the cocktail stick and if they hold it directly overhead the shadow disappears. This page could be linked with numeracy – measuring accurately in centimetres.

Resources: cocktail stick ● Plasticine ● torch

> **Vocabulary:** *beam, block, cast, darkness, light, longer, shadow, shorter.*

Compass points (page 60) prepares the children for the subsequent activities in this section by helping them to understand what is meant by *north, south, west* and *east,* and that these directions never change. Many children think that north is in whichever direction the 'N' on the compass happens to point. Discuss this; point out that if this were true they could change 'north' by turning a compass round, but that north is always in the same place. You could show them a globe and help them to find the North and South Poles. Some children might make links between this and their previous work on magnets. If so, it might be useful to explain that a compass needle is a magnet, with a north and south pole (they are actually north- and south-*seeking* poles, but it is not necessary to explain this unless any of the children would benefit from it). You could show them what happens when a magnet, resting horizontally in a piece of paper, is suspended from a piece of string (its north pole swings towards the direction of north). Make sure the compasses are working properly. They should be kept away from magnets.

Resources: compasses

> **Vocabulary:** *compass, direction, east, north, point, pole, south, west.*

Shadow stick: 1 and **2** (pages 61–62) shows that shadows change in size and position throughout the day and that the position of the Sun in the sky causes these changes. The Warn the children never to look at the Sun; it damages the eyes. *Be Safe!* provides guidance on working with the Sun and shadows. weather need not be brilliantly sunny as long as *some* shadows are produced. If desired, you could use a much larger object for producing shadows, for example, a plastic bottle filled with sand. Take a compass outside and help the children to mark the directions on the ground. When they mark the shadow they should mark the time when it is observed. If the shadow stick has to be taken up after each observation, a mark should be made on the ground so that it can be put back in the same place each time. These records could be made on a large sheet of paper kept in place with weights such as heavy stones; this could be kept as a record and displayed in the classroom, perhaps in conjunction with a numeracy project on using directions and time. After completing these activities you could help the children to track the changes in position of the Sun across a classroom window (if you have a south-facing window). The Sun is at its highest point at midday, but the adjustment of British Summer Time has to be taken into account.

> **Vocabulary:** *compass, diagram, direction, east, hour, length, measure, midday, noon, north, point, pole, shadow, south, time, west.*

Shadow clock (page 63) shows how the lengths of shadows can be used to tell the approximate time of day. It would fit in well with numeracy lessons on telling the Warn the children never to look at the Sun; it damages the eyes. time. Provide the children with examples (or pictures) of different types of sundial and discuss how they work. Most are based on the positions of the shadows, but this model is simpler. The children will find that some of the times they mark are in similar places. Ask them if they can explain this; remind them of their previous work on the lengths of shadows at different times of the day.

> **Vocabulary:** *clock, hour, length, longer, shadow, shorter, time.*

Shadow patterns (page 64) helps to demonstrate that transparent materials let light through, but opaque materials do not. The children use their knowledge about light and shadows to predict which materials will form shadows and to compare the shadows formed by different materials, from a thick, opaque material like wood to a thin, semi-transparent material like voile. They could make a large chart and glue on samples of the materials tested. They can contribute more as they come across and test other materials. You could also relate this activity to work on prefixes (*trans-*) and opposites (*dark/light, opaque/transparent*) in literacy.

> **Vocabulary:** *block, blurred, darkness, light, opaque, shadow, sharp, translucent, transparent.*

Shopping basket: 1

Understand that all animals, including humans, need to feed

Bananas, Biscuits, Sugar, Butter, Chicken, Apples, Carrots, Cabbage, Fish fingers, Lentils, Chocolate, Cake, Cream, Milk, Melon, Ice cream, Tuna, Sausages, Peanuts, Honey, Avocado, Bread, Cheese, Yogurt, Sunflower seeds, Cornflakes, Beefburgers, Olive oil

Teachers' note Use this with page 13. Ask the children what animals need in order to stay alive. What do people need? Remind them that people are animals. Review what they know about all animals' need for food and water. Tell them that there are different types of food and that foods can be grouped with other similar foods.

Developing Science
Year 3
© A & C BLACK

Shopping basket: 2

- ## Put the shopping in the cupboard.
- ## Write the words.

Meat and fish

Dairy foods

Fruit and vegetables

Pulses, nuts and seeds

Fats

Sugars and starches

Now try this!

- ## Add another food to each shelf.

Teachers' note Use this with page 12. Give out pictures of different foods and ask the children to sort them into groups. Discuss the groupings. Read the heading on each cupboard shelf and ask the children to find a food of that type in the shopping basket. Children should start by choosing to allocate a food to just one group. Some children might notice that some foods belong to more than one group.

Developing Science
Year 3
© **A & C BLACK**

Fit to eat

Understand that animals need to feed to grow and to be active

Foods help our bodies in different ways:

Foods that help us to grow

yogurt

lentils

beans

cheese

fish

meat

Foods that help us to be active

pasta

biscuits

bread

cake

honey

- **Draw and label a meal that helps you to grow and be active.**

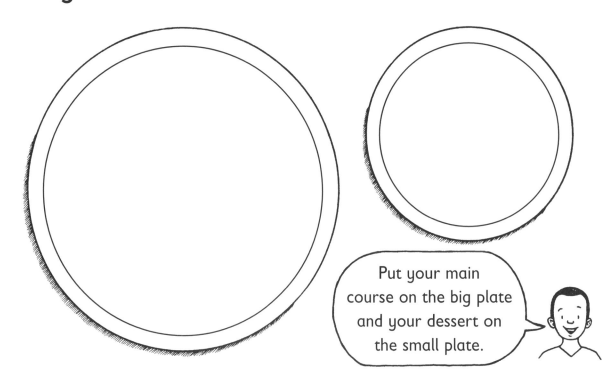

Put your main course on the big plate and your dessert on the small plate.

Now try this!

- **Draw another group of foods that help your body to stay healthy.**

Teachers' note The children should first have completed pages 12–13. Explain that our bodies use different foods in different ways: some help our bodies to grow and replace worn parts (for example, our skin is being renewed all the time), others give us energy for action. Read the names of the foods for each purpose. Ask the children to think of others.

Developing Science
Year 3
© **A & C BLACK**

Food for thought

Recognise that we need a varied diet to stay healthy

• **Write letters from the key in the boxes to help people with special** diets **to choose a meal.**

For some foods you might need to write more than one letter.

Key

F – contains fish
M – contains meat
N – contains nuts
V – vegetarian

Menu

Starters

☐ Pea and ham soup

☐ Pickled herrings

☐ Tomato salad: tomato, onion and parsley

Main courses

☐ Haddock, chips and peas

☐ Fried lamb's liver with gravy and mashed potatoes

☐ Stuffed tomatoes: large tomatoes stuffed with mixed nuts and herbs

Pizzas

☐ Marguerita: mozzarella cheese, onion, tomato

☐ Roma special: mozzarella cheese, ham, spiced sausage

Desserts

☐ Apple pie and custard

☐ Raspberries with vanilla yogurt

☐ Mixed fruit salad: pineapple, peach, pear, plum, strawberries

☐ Apricot delight: apricot purée topped with chopped almonds

Now try this!

• **Find out what** vegans **eat.**

• **Write the letter P in the boxes to help vegans choose a meal.**

Teachers' note The children should first have completed pages 12–14. Give each group a collection of menus and ask them to look for foods from the groups identified on page 13. Introduce and explain the word *diet*. Can the children think of any special diets some people have (see page 5)? Why do they follow these diets?

Developing Science
Year 3
© A & C BLACK

15

Dog's dinner

Present evidence about animals' foods in a bar chart

- **Use the** bar chart **to record your findings about what dogs eat.**

There is space to add other foods.

Number of dogs (y-axis: 14, 13, 12, 11, 10, 9, 8, 7, 6, 5, 4, 3, 2, 1, 0)

Foods (x-axis): Tripe, Tinned dog food, Rabbit

Which food is eaten by the greatest number of dogs?

_____

Why do you think this is?

_____
_____
_____
_____
_____
_____
_____
_____
_____
_____
_____

Now try this!

- **Write what you could do to find out whether dogs eat the foods they like best.**

Teachers' note For homework prior to this activity, ask the children to find out what foods are eaten by dogs belonging to their friends or family. Discuss how they can record the numbers of dogs that eat particular foods. Ask the children if their investigation helps them to answer questions such as: 'Do all dogs eat meat?', 'Do all dogs like meat?', 'Do dogs like some foods better than others?' Discuss how they can find the answers to questions with which the graph does not help.

Developing Science
Year 3
© A & C BLACK

Food watch

Turn ideas about animals' diets into an investigation

• Find out what a snail chooses to eat.

① Set out some foods like this:

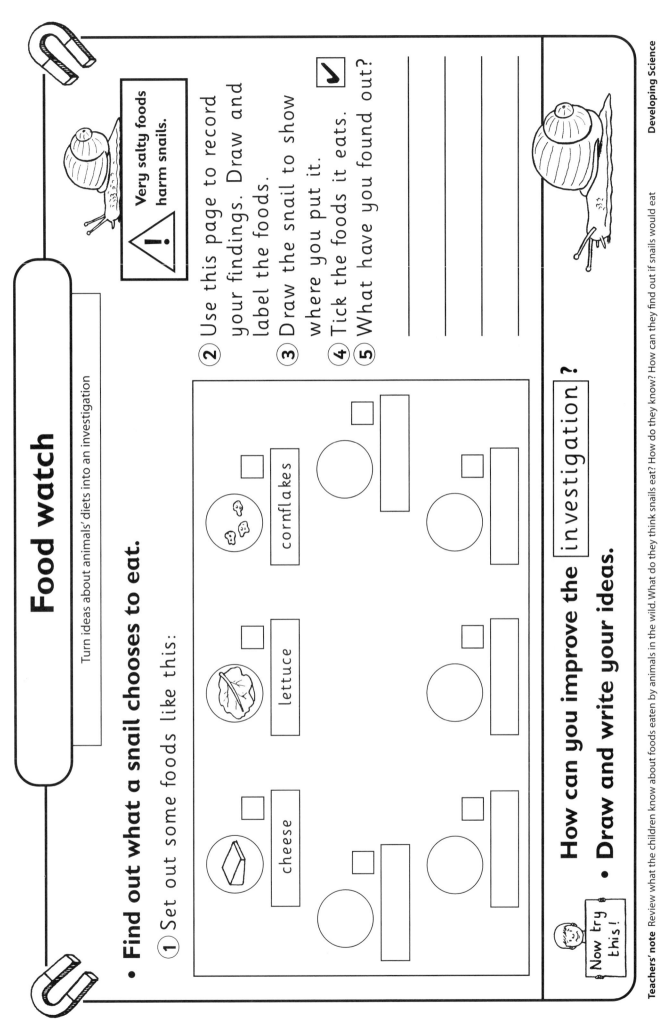

cheese

lettuce

cornflakes

② Use this page to record your findings. Draw and label the foods.

③ Draw the snail to show where you put it.

④ Tick the foods it eats.

⑤ What have you found out?

⚠️ **Very salty foods harm snails.**

• How can you improve the investigation ?
• Draw and write your ideas.

Now try this!

Teachers' note Review what the children know about foods eaten by animals in the wild. What do they think snails eat? How do they know? How can they find out if snails would eat other foods given the chance? Discuss foods that can be offered to snails: biscuits, cheese, chocolate, cornflakes, cucumber, raw porridge oats, salad and vegetable leaves, but nothing very salty such as crisps. The children could predict which foods a snail will eat. Discuss how to make the test fair (see page 5).

Developing Science
Year 3
© A & C BLACK

Our teeth

Understand that we have two sets of teeth

- Look at your teeth and record them on the diagram.

Colour `milk teeth` green. Colour `second teeth` red.
Leave missing teeth blank.

Top

front

back

back

front

Bottom.

	Top	Bottom
Front		
Back		

Where are most of your second teeth? ✔

Now try this!

- Find out where your group's second teeth are.

- Write the numbers of teeth:
(No. is short for number)

	Top		Bottom	
	Tally	No.	Tally	No.
Front				
Back				

Teachers' note Provide the children with mirrors and ask them to look at their teeth. Have any of their teeth come out? Introduce the terms *milk teeth* and *second teeth*. Show the children how to record their teeth on the diagram. Begin at the front of the top teeth and work towards the back on one side, then repeat for the other side. Repeat for the bottom teeth.

Developing Science
Year 3
© A & C BLACK

A bite to eat

- **Match the descriptions to the teeth.**
- **Match the teeth to what they are used for.**

Draw lines to match them.

Descriptions	Teeth	Used for
pointed	incisors	chewing
broad and flat	canines	cutting and biting
with a narrow, flat edge	molars	tearing

- **Find the different teeth in your mouth:**

Description	Used for	Front or back	Number

Now try this!

Which teeth do you use when you:
- bite into an apple? _____
- tear a piece off the apple? _____
- chew the piece of apple? _____

Teachers' note The children should first have completed page 18. Discuss the shapes of their teeth and ask them to point out the different types of teeth they have. If possible, provide an apple for each child to eat and ask them which teeth they use to bite into it (incisors), to tear off a piece (canines) and then to chew it (molars). Name the different types of teeth.

Developing Science
Year 3
© A & C BLACK

19

A toothy tale

Understand that our adult teeth have to last

What will happen next?

• Draw and write the ending of each story.

Nina had a wobbly tooth.	She pulled out the wobbly tooth.
Dad had toothache.	The tooth was too bad to fill. The dentist took it out.

 Now try this!

• Explain to a partner why we need to take special care of adult teeth.

Teachers' note Invite the children to share their experiences of loose teeth and how they came out. Draw attention to what made the tooth come out; usually it is loosened by an adult tooth growing beneath it, pushing the milk tooth out of its way. Discuss what happens when an adult loses a tooth (also discuss what else can be done if an adult tooth is damaged).

Developing Science
Year 3
© A & C BLACK

A healthy smile

Recognise that some foods can damage our teeth

This game is for two to four players.

- **Take turns to roll the die and move your counter.**

You need

a die

a counter each

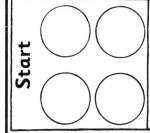

Start

You brushed your teeth after supper.
Move on 2.

You shared your toothbrush with a friend.
Go back 2.

You ate an apple.
Move on 1.

You have a new toothbrush.
Move on 1.

You went to bed without brushing your teeth.
Go back 5.

You drank a glass of milk.
Move on 2.

You have been eating toffees all afternoon.
Go back 4.

You ate some chocolate after lunch but you rinsed out your mouth.
Move on 1.

You have not had a dental check-up for 2 years.
Go back 3.

You have brushed your teeth twice a day for 5 days.
Move on 5.

Finish

Now try this!

- **Write three sentences about how you look after your** teeth .

Teachers' note Display posters and provide leaflets about tooth care and, if possible, show the children a video or arrange for a dental health specialist to talk to the children about caring for their teeth. Draw the children's attention to foods that help to keep the teeth and gums healthy (see page 6). The game can be used to assess what they have learned.

Developing Science
Year 3
© A & C BLACK

Harvest time

Recognise that plants can provide food

Which foods do you think come from |plants|?

- **Write on the chart.**
- **Find out if you were right.**

Use information books.

Food	Do you think it is from a plant?	What did you find out?
beef		
butter		
coffee		
flour		
peanut		
prawn		
salt		
sugar		
tea		

Now try this!

- **Find out how one of the foods is grown, collected or made.**
- **Make notes and then write a report about it.**

Teachers' note Review the children's previous learning about foods from plants. If possible, take them to an allotment, market garden, greengrocery or supermarket. Name and discuss different plants grown for food (including processed foods made from plants). Ask the children to find out about plants that are treated in some way before they are eaten, and those that are combined with other ingredients in foods.

Developing Science
Year 3
© **A & C BLACK**

The leaf thief

Understand that plants need leaves to grow well

The leaf thief thinks that plants can manage without their | leaves |**. So she steals them.**

About how many of a plant's leaves do you think it is safe to take off? ✔

none ☐   a few ☐   about half of them ☐

most of them ☐   all of them ☐

How can you find out?

This is what I need:

_____

_____

_____

_____

This is what I shall do:

_____

_____

_____

_____

_____

For each plant I shall keep these things the same:

_____

_____

_____

I shall change only this:

_____

If I am right, this is what will happen:

_____

_____

_____

_____

Teachers' note Ask the children if all plants have leaves. Show them a collection of plants and ask them to identify the leaves. What are the leaves for? Discuss how they can find out if plants need leaves to grow well. They could share their experiences of plants (for example, what happens if a leaf falls off or when shrubs are pruned). As an extension activity, ask them to examine leaves with a magnifying glass and to explain what they think leaves are for.

Developing Science
Year 3
© **A & C BLACK**

Rooted to the spot

Observe and measure growing plants

• Observe and record the growth of two plants.

Plant 1 is in a pot that is too small.

Weeks 1 2 3 4

Height in centimetres

Plant 2 is in a bigger pot.

Weeks 1 2 3 4

Height in centimetres

What else can you observe each week?
• Write notes about each plant.

Now try this!

Teachers' note Show the children the roots of a plant that has outgrown its pot and of another that does not fill its pot. Ask them if they think it makes any difference to a plant if it is grown in a small or a large pot. How can they find out? Review what they know about fair tests. Establish that they should observe the growth of plants of the same type and similar size (see also page 6). The numbers on the vertical axis of the graph have been omitted so that you can insert a suitable scale.

Developing Science
Year 3
© **A & C BLACK**

Sucking it up

Understand that water flows through the stem to other parts of a plant

- **Put a stick of celery into a pot of coloured water.**
- **Record your observations in the boxes.**
- **Start at the bottom of the page.**
- **Draw lines to link the boxes to the celery.**

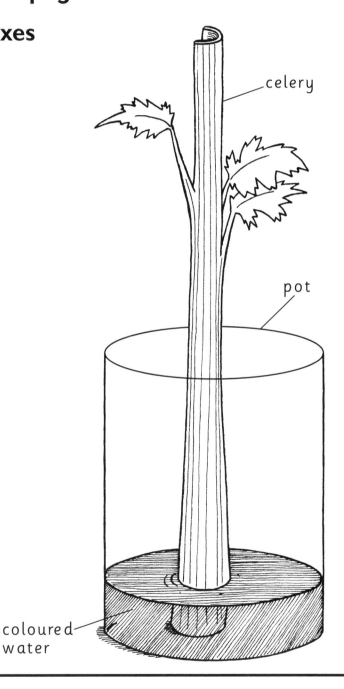

celery

pot

coloured water

After _____ minutes

After _____ minutes

After _____ minutes

After 20 minutes

After 10 minutes

Now try this!

- **Write what you have learned about how water travels to different parts of a plant.**

Teachers' note The children should first have completed page 24. Show the children a complete head of celery and draw their attention to the stems. Cut off the stems and give them to the children to observe. Provide magnifying glasses so they can see the holes in the end of the stem. Stand the celery stalks in a small amount of dyed water and ask the children what they think will happen to the water. Where will it go? (See also page 6.)

Developing Science
Year 3
© **A & C BLACK**

Enough water: 1

Understand that plants need water, but not unlimited water

**Will a seedling grow better
the more ⎡water⎤ you give it?**

How can you find out?

a seedling

Our question:

We need:

_____

_____

_____

_____

_____

What we shall do:

_____

_____

_____

_____

_____

_____

What we shall keep the same
for each seedling:

_____

_____

_____

_____

What we shall change
for each seedling:

_____

_____

_____

_____

What we shall measure:

_____

_____

What we shall record:

_____

_____

26

Teachers' note The children should first have completed pages 23–25. Ask the children if they think that a plant will grow better if it is given more water. Show them some seedlings (for example, marigolds, cress or beans) and ask the children how they can find out if a plant grows better the more water it is given. As an extension, they could make and explain predictions about what will happen. Continued on pages 27–28.

**Developing Science
Year 3**
© A & C BLACK

Enough water: 2

Measure volume of water and height of plant

• Record what happens to seedlings given different amounts of ☐water☐ each day.

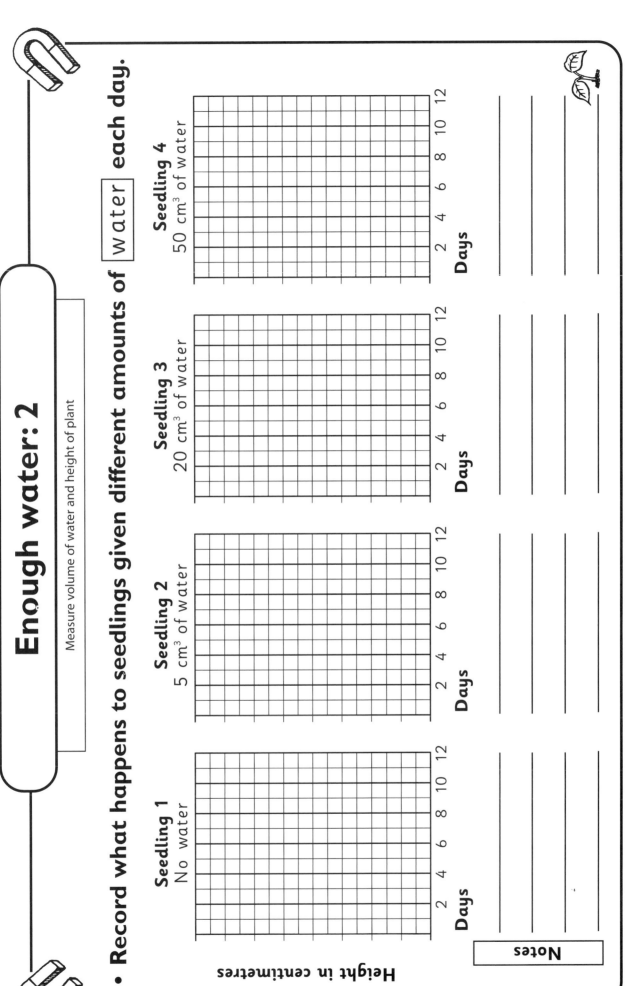

Seedling 1
No water

Seedling 2
5 cm³ of water

Seedling 3
20 cm³ of water

Seedling 4
50 cm³ of water

Days

Days

Days

Days

Height in centimetres

Notes

_____

_____

_____

Teachers' note The children should first have completed page 26. Discuss the children's ideas for investigating the question of whether a seedling grows better the more water it is given and discuss the amounts of water to give it and how to measure the water. Explain how the bar chart should be completed and what other observations to record (for example, the colour of the seedling and how strong the stem looks). The numbers on the vertical axis of the graph have been omitted so that you can insert a suitable scale.

Developing Science
Year 3
© A & C BLACK

Enough water: 3

Decide how much evidence is needed to judge the growth of a seedling

- **Look at the seedlings you investigated.**
- **Look at the results you recorded.**
- **Draw the seedlings in order:**

| unhealthiest | ⟶ | healthiest |

Seedling ☐	Seedling ☐	Seedling ☐	Seedling ☐
Water per day	Water per day	Water per day	Water per day

What is the answer to your question?

_____

_____

_____

Write a sentence.

Why do you think this is? _____

_____

_____

_____

Now try this!

How could you improve your investigation?
- **Write what you could do.**

Teachers' note The children should first have completed pages 26–27. After about 12 days of growing, watering, measuring and observing the seedlings, ask the children what they have found out from their results. They should be able to decide which are the most healthy and which the least healthy seedlings and to order them accordingly. Discuss how they could improve the investigation (see page 6).

Developing Science
Year 3
© A & C BLACK

In the dark: 1

Understand that plants need light for healthy growth

Leanne and Meera want to find out what happens when grass has no `sunlight` **.**

I'm going to put two bricks onto a patch of grass.

Leanne

I'm going to put an upturned bucket onto a patch of grass.

Meera

Whose idea is the better, and why? _____

_____

_____

How long should she leave the grass covered?

_____

How often should she observe it? _____

_____

What else should she observe and why? _____

_____

_____

_____

_____

Now try this!

- **Write a plan for Leanne's or Meera's investigation.**

Teachers' note Discuss the children's experience of grass that has been left covered for some time. What does it look like? Talk about how bricks and an upturned bucket might affect the growth of grass they are left standing on. How can the children compare this with uncovered grass? See also page 30.

Developing Science
Year 3
© A & C BLACK

In the dark: 2

Suggest how a fair test can be carried out

What happens to grass that has been kept in the dark when you uncover it?

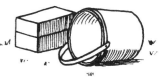

_____

Will it be the same for other plants? _____

• Plan an investigation to find out.

My question:

_____

I need:	I shall do this:
_____	_____
_____	_____
_____	_____
_____	_____

I shall keep these things the same for each plant:	I shall change only this:
_____	_____
_____	_____
_____	_____
_____	_____

I shall observe and measure:

_____

If I am right, this is what will happen:

_____

_____

Teachers' note The children should first have completed page 29. Ask them if they think the grass that has been covered will die or if it will grow again if it is uncovered. Discuss how long they should leave the grass covered and what they will observe, measure and record after they uncover it (for example, height, colour and whether it begins to grow upright again). As an extension, the children could write explanations for their findings.

Developing Science
Year 3
© A & C BLACK

Hothouse plants

Understand that plant growth is affected by temperature

A hothouse or greenhouse is a warm place for plants.

Alankar and Jane wanted to find out if plants grow better in warm **places.**

We put a geranium, planted in soil, on a window ledge near a radiator.

Then we planted some cress seeds on blotting paper and put them in the fridge.

Alankar

Jane

What is wrong with Alankar and Jane's investigation?

1 _____

_____

2 _____

_____

3 _____

_____

4 _____

_____

Now try this!

- **Plan a better investigation for Alankar and Jane.**
- **Write instructions to tell them what to do.**

Teachers' note If possible, take the children into a greenhouse, or ask them about their experiences of greenhouses. Why do people grow plants in them? What difference do they make? Discuss how they can find out whether heat makes a difference to the growth of plants. Ask them to think about what to keep the same and what to change for each plant.

Developing Science
Year 3
© A & C BLACK

Material world

- **Look around your school.**

  What are things made of?

  Can they be made of other materials?

Object	Material	What else can it be made of?
door		
door handle		
drain pipe		
electrical socket		
fence		
floor (indoor)		
floor (outdoor)		
window frame		
window pane		

- **Choose three objects from the chart.**
- **Explain why the materials are suitable.**

Teachers' note This activity is intended as a starting point for work on materials. Take the children to look at objects around the school, particularly the materials from which parts of the building are made. Help them to identify and describe the materials and ask them from what else the objects can be made. Some children might be able to explain why certain materials are suitable for these purposes; others could say which materials would be unsuitable.

Developing Science
Year 3
© A & C BLACK

A closer look

Recognise that materials are used because of their properties

- **Write what is good** 😊 **and bad** 😞 **about each of these** materials **for making a drinking cup.**

Ceramics

😊 _____

😞 _____

Glass

😊 _____

😞 _____

Plastic

😊 _____

😞 _____

Metal

😊 _____

😞 _____

- **Draw and write about another object that can be made of different materials.**

😊 _____

😞 _____

😊 _____

😞 _____

😊 _____

😞 _____

😊 _____

😞 _____

Now try this!

- **Choose an object from the classroom.**
- **Draw it and write what it is made of. Explain why you think it is made of that material.**

Teachers' note The children should first have completed page 32. Remind them of the words they used in their descriptions of materials. Show them a collection of mugs made of different materials and invite them to comment on what makes each material good for a mug. They could also comment on any drawbacks of the material. Introduce the words *advantage* and *disadvantage*.

Developing Science
Year 3
© A & C BLACK

Guess which material?

Recognising properties of materials

Which |material| **is this?**

It is hard. It breaks if you drop it on a hard surface. It is opaque.

Word-bank

bendy	hard
break	opaque
crumple	soft
flexible	strong
fold	translucent
fragile	transparent

Answer: _____

- **Write descriptions of other materials.**
- **Give them to others in your group to guess.**

It is bendy. It _____

_____

_____

_____

_____

_____

_____

_____

_____

_____

_____

_____

_____

_____

Teachers' note The children should first have completed pages 32–33. Put a material sample in a box and give the children one clue at a time until they work out what it is. Include ceramics, fabrics, glass, leather, metal, plastic, rubber, stone, wood. Introduce adjectives to describe them (see page 7). As an extension, some children could make a materials guessing game, devising questions to be answered by a partner who has chosen a material: for example, 'Is it bendy?', 'Is it hard?'.

Developing Science
Year 3
© **A & C BLACK**

Splat test

When you drop a ball of Plasticine onto a hard surface it goes 'splat'! One side is flattened.

- **Try it!**
- **Measure the splat like this:**
    - **Draw round the splat.**
    - **Count the squares.**
- **Test different surfaces.**

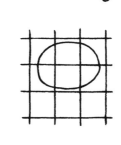

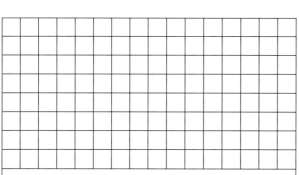

Surface	Splat size
concrete	_____ squares

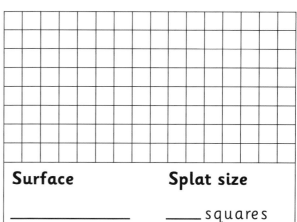

Surface	Splat size
_____	_____ squares

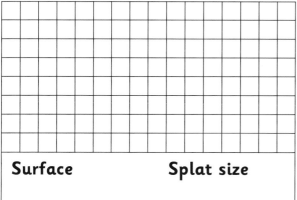

Surface	Splat size
_____	_____ squares

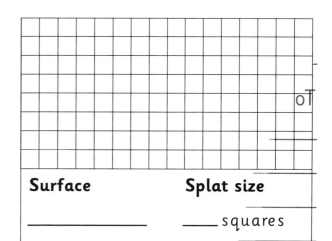

Surface	Splat size
_____	_____ squares

Now try this!

- **Explain how you made your test** fair **.**
- **Write about how you can improve your test.**

Teachers' note The children should first have completed pages 32–34. Discuss how they know if a material is hard. Invite them to drop a ball of soft Plasticine onto the floor and to observe how it changes. Does the same happen on all floors? Encourage the children to compare the effects of a hard floor such as vinyl and a soft one such as carpet. Which makes the Plasticine 'splat' the most? Discuss how it can be used to test the hardness of a material and how to make the test fair.

Developing Science
Year 3
A & C BLACK

Tough stuff

- **Look at these materials.**

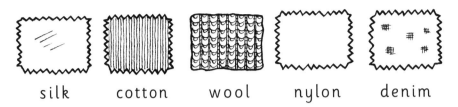

silk   cotton   wool   nylon   denim

Susie

Which fabric should be used to patch the knees of Susie's jeans? _____

- **Plan a test to find the most hardwearing fabric.**

This is what I shall do: _____

_____

_____

_____

You could rub each fabric until you make a hole in it.

I shall need: _____

_____

_____

How will you hold the fabric? What will you rub it on?

To make the test fair I shall _____

_____

_____

Will you time how long you take? Or will you count the rubs?

How will you make each rub the same?

Now try this!

- **Tell a friend what you will measure and how you will record your results.**

Teachers' note The children should first have completed pages 32–35. Discuss how they know if a material is hardwearing and what this means. The samples of fabric could be wrapped around a stone and rubbed on a rough surface such as concrete or paving stones until a hole appears. The children need to find a way to measure the amount of rubbing needed to make a hole (see page 7).

Developing Science Year 3
© A & C BLACK

Soak it up: 1

Plan a test to compare the absorbency of different papers

Which paper do you think is the most | absorbent | ?

- Cut out some samples, glue them here in order and label them.

Predict.

least absorbent ⟶ most absorbent

- Collect some other, bigger samples to test.

How can you measure how much water they will soak up?

Now try this!

- See if you can improve your test.
- Write what you did.

Teachers' note The children should first have completed pages 32–36. Let them handle different types of paper and examine them with magnifying glasses. Tell them the names of the papers. Introduce the word *absorbent* and discuss its meaning. Can they think of any absorbent materials (for example, sponge, towelling)? How can they tell if a material will be absorbent by handling it and looking closely at it? See also page 38.

Developing Science
Year 3
© A & C BLACK

Soak it up: 2

Measure the absorbency of different papers

● Record how much water different types of paper soak up.

Colour the drops.

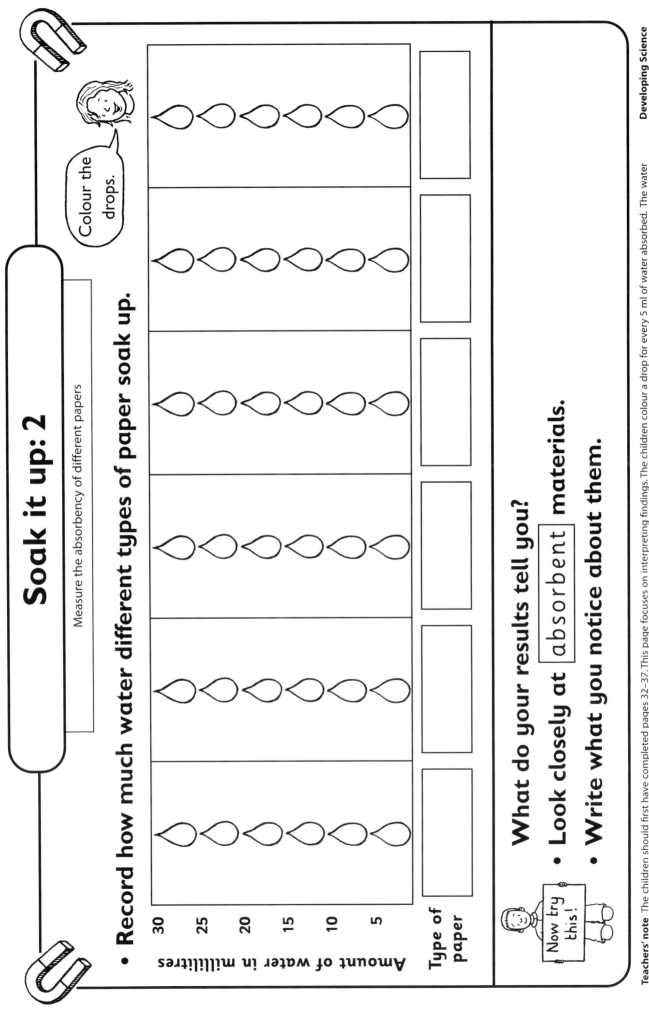

Amount of water in millilitres

30
25
20
15
10
5

Type of paper

What do your results tell you?

● Look closely at absorbent materials.

● Write what you notice about them.

Now try this!

Teachers' note The children should first have completed pages 32–37. This page focuses on interpreting findings. The children colour a drop for every 5 ml of water absorbed. The water could be measured in spoonfuls; if so, change the vertical axis of the graph. They can glue labelled samples of each paper at the foot of each column of the bar chart. They should be able to tell at a glance which is the most absorbent by the number of drops they have coloured. Ask them to use their results to check if their predictions on page 37 were right.

Developing Science
Year 3
© A & C BLACK

Evaluate tests for stretchiness

How can you measure how stretchy a pair of tights is?

- **Write improvements for these tests. Make them fair.**

I shall stand on the feet of the tights and pull the top. Someone can measure them.

_____

_____

_____

_____

_____

Put some stones in the feet of the tights. Lift the tights by the top. Measure the stretch.

_____

_____

_____

_____

_____

Now try this!

- **Write how you will measure the stretch of tights.**
  - **What will you do?**
  - **What will you need?**
  - **How will you make the test fair?**
  - **What will you observe and measure?**

Teachers' note The children should first have completed pages 32–38. Give the children a collection of materials and ask them to put them in order according to how stretchy they are. How can they tell if something is stretchy? Discuss how stretchiness can be measured and introduce the words _elastic_ and _elasticity_. For what objects is this quality useful, and why?

Developing Science
Year 3
© A & C BLACK

Suit yourself

Understand that some properties are more important than others

- **Imagine you are an inventor who has to make a new** material **for a swimsuit.**

This is no good. It's transparent!

- **Describe what the material should be like.**

My new swimsuit fabric should be

_____

_____

_____

_____

The most important quality is

_____

- **Write instructions for testing this quality.**

Word-bank

absorbent

hardwearing

opaque

quick-drying

stretchy

strong

translucent

transparent

washable

waterproof

Do this:	You need:
_____	_____
_____	_____
_____	_____
_____	_____

Keep these things the same:

Measure:

Record:

Teachers' note The children should first have completed pages 32–39. Provide a collection of swimsuits for the children to examine. Ask them to describe the materials from which they are made. Encourage them to identify properties such as those listed in the word-bank and to say which are important. Properties for the children to test could include elasticity, how quickly it dries, strength, whether it remains opaque when wet.

Developing Science
Year 3
© **A & C BLACK**

All kinds of rocks

Observe and compare rocks

You need some samples of rock:

 chalk

 granite

 limestone

 pumice

 quartz

 sandstone

 slate

Think about colour, pattern and texture.

• Describe the rocks:

Rock	Description

* Read your description of a rock aloud to a friend.
* Ask your friend to guess which rock it is.

Now try this!

Word-bank

black
brown
dull
flat
grey
holes
matt
orange
pink
ridges
rough
sharp
shiny
smooth
speckled
white

Teachers' note Give each group a collection of miscellaneous rocks and ask them to sort them into groups of the same kind. Invite them to explain how they sorted them. Ask others to work out how they have sorted them). Introduce words for describing rocks (see page 8), as well as words such as *pebble* and *boulder*.

Developing Science
Year 3
© A & C BLACK

Hard as rock

Test differences between rocks

- **Test the** hardness **of rocks.**

- **Try to scratch each rock with:
your fingernail, a coin, a nail-file, a nail.**

You need

a 2p coin

a nail-file

a nail (about 5 cm long)

samples of different rocks

You may need a harder scratcher.

- **Record your findings.
What scratched it?** ✔

Rock	Fingernail	Coin	Nail-file	Nail

Now try this!

- **Draw the rocks in order of hardness.**

Teachers' note Provide the children with samples of the same rocks they described for page 41 and ask them which they think is the hardest. How can they tell? Ensure that they understand that hardness refers to how easily the rock can be damaged by scratching. They could then try scratching each rock with the different implements listed (including their fingernails). The fewer the implements that will scratch it, the harder the rock is.

Developing Science
Year 3
© **A & C BLACK**

Passing through

Test differences between rocks

Will water soak into these rocks? ✔ or ✘

chalk ☐   granite ☐   limestone ☐

pumice ☐   sandstone ☐   slate ☐

How can you find out? _____

_____

_____

What will you observe? _____

_____

_____

• **Test the rocks, and record your results here:**

_____

_____

_____

_____

_____

_____

• **Write what will happen when it rains on a field on** chalk **and a field on** slate .

Teachers' note Provide the children with samples of rocks they described for page 41 and ask them through which rock they think water will soak the most easily, and why. Remind them that there is rock beneath the ground everywhere, and ask them how the type of rock might affect what happens to any rainfall and any streams flowing across the ground.

Developing Science
Year 3
© A & C BLACK

Hard facts

Identify which rocks are suitable for particular purposes

- **Find out about the useful** $\boxed{\text{rocks}}$ **listed on the chart.**

  What makes them good $\boxed{\text{materials}}$ **for these uses?**

Examine the rock samples and read about them in books.

Rock	Use	Why is it good for this use?
chalk	Writing on a hard surface	
granite	Kerbstones	
limestone	Making cement	
pumice	Rubbing off hard, dead skin	
quartz	Working watches and other electronic machines	
sandstone	Building blocks for walls	
slate	Roof tiles	

Now try this!

- **Write a report about one of the rocks, using the information on this page.**
- **Find out where more information about rocks can be found.**

Use information books.

Teachers' note Provide the children with samples of rocks they described for page 41 and discuss some of the uses of these rocks. You could describe other uses of rocks (for example, sandstone as 'donkey stones' in the past, for scrubbing steps) and ask them what might make the rocks suitable for these uses. Provide reference materials: information books and CD-ROMs (see the notes for page 41 on page 8).

Developing Science
Year 3
© **A & C BLACK**

Bits and pieces

- **Observe each** soil **sample.**

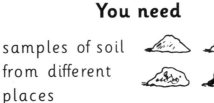

You need

samples of soil from different places

a magnifying glass

three riddles

- **Notice the shapes, sizes and colours of the pieces.**

- **Draw the soil samples.**

small holes   medium holes   big holes

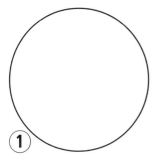 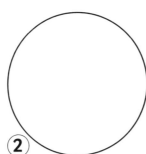 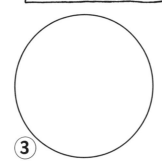 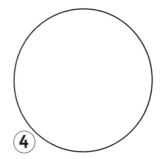

① ② ③ ④

- **Use riddles to find out which soil has the biggest pieces.**

- **Fill in the chart.**

Soil	Riddles passed through		
	big holes	medium holes	small holes
1			
2			
3			
4			

Which is the finest soil?

Now try this!

- **Describe and record the feel of each soil:**

gritty   sharp   silky

Teachers' note The children should first have completed pages 41–44. Provide them with samples of soil from areas based on different rocks. They should have different textures and colours. Encourage the children to describe what they see when they examine the soils. Point out that soils are made up mainly of bits of rock. They could use riddles, sieves, or plastic pots whose bases have been pierced with holes of different sizes.

Developing Science
Year 3
© A & C BLACK

Waterlogged: 1

It has been raining, but now it has stopped.

Kim's garden has dried.

Joe's garden is waterlogged.

'Our gardens must have different types of soil,' said Kim.

They planned a test to measure how well water soaked into each type of soil.

- **Read the test and underline anything that makes it unfair.**

Kim shovelled some of her soil into a bucket with holes in the bottom. She turned the hosepipe onto it. Lots of water soaked through.

Joe put a spoonful of his soil into a yogurt pot with holes in the bottom. Then he poured on some water. None soaked through.

Now try this!

- **Write a letter to Kim and Joe to explain what is wrong with their test.**

Teachers' note The children should first have completed page 45. Point out that the soil, as well as the rock beneath it, affects the drainage of the land. If possible, take the children out after it has rained to observe which places dry quickly and which stay wet. Discuss where some of the water goes. Continued on page 47.

Developing Science
Year 3
© A & C BLACK

Waterlogged: 2

Plan a fair test; measure time and volume

Which of these soils do you think Kim **and** Joe **have in their gardens?**

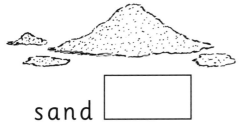

sand ☐

clay ☐

Why do you think this? _____

_____

_____

- **Plan a fair test to compare sand and clay:**

My question:

_____

I shall do this:	I shall need these:
_____	_____
_____	_____
_____	_____
_____	_____

I shall keep these things the same for each soil:

_____

I shall change only this:

_____

I shall observe and measure these:

_____

Teachers' note The children should first have completed page 45. Before they begin, ensure that they can say what they are trying to find out and how this will help them to decide what kind of soil Kim and Joe have in their gardens (page 46). Remind them of their observations about soils and encourage them to relate the results of their test to the characteristics of the soil. This could also be linked with previous learning about absorbent materials.

Developing Science
Year 3
© **A & C BLACK**

Poles apart

Understand that magnets attract or repel each other

• **Draw what happens next:**

① ② ③

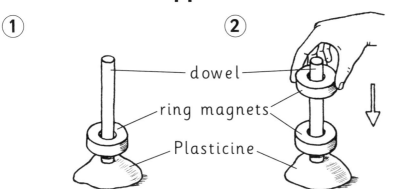
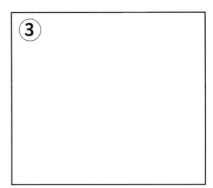

- dowel
- ring magnets
- Plasticine

Does this always happen? _____

• **Draw what happens next:**

① ②

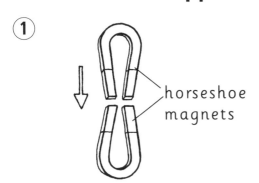
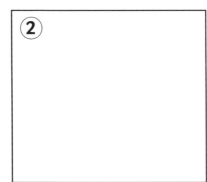

horseshoe magnets

Does this always happen?

_____

• **Draw what happens if you push two bar magnets together.**

Now try this!

• **Fix magnets onto two toy cars to stop them crashing when you roll them gently towards each other.**

• **Record what happens.**

Teachers' note Provide a collection of magnets and ask the children to explore what happens when they put magnets next to one another. Tell them to try them side by side or end to end. Encourage them to describe what they observe and feel happening, and introduce the words *attract* and *repel*.

Developing Science
Year 3
© A & C BLACK

Magnet puzzles

Predict and test whether materials are magnetic or not

- **Predict:**

  Will you be able to use a $\boxed{\text{magnet}}$ **to separate these objects or materials?** $\boxed{\text{Yes}}$ **or** $\boxed{\text{No}}$

Objects or materials	Prediction	Reason	✔
paper clips and drawing pins			
nails and screws			
sugar and salt			
drinks cans and dog food cans			
recording tape and ribbon			
wooden and plastic blocks			
gold and silver jewellery			

Now try this!

- **Use a magnet to check your predictions.**
- **For which ones were you right?** $\boxed{✔}$
- **Write what you have learned about metals.**

Teachers' note The children should first have completed page 48. Show them a box containing a mixture of pins and buttons. Ask them to think of an easy way to separate them without having to pick out each object separately. Discuss why a magnet would be useful. Invite one of the children to demonstrate. Ask them to decide which of the mixtures on this page can be separated using a magnet and why (or why not).

Developing Science
Year 3
© A & C BLACK

Everyday magnets

Recognise that magnets have a variety of uses

- **Find out how** magnets **are used in or on everyday things.**
- **Record your findings on the chart.**

Object	What the magnet does
memory board	
board game	
cassette recorder	
cupboard	
fridge	

- **Draw and write about something else in which a magnet would be useful.**

Teachers' note Provide objects containing magnets for the children to explore: for example, magnetic board games, fasteners on bags and cases, tailors' magnets/pin containers and fridge magnets (tell them also that cupboard doors and fridge doors sometimes contain magnets to keep them closed). Discuss how the magnets are useful and ask the children about other useful magnets they have seen.

Developing Science
Year 3
© **A & C BLACK**

Strong magnets: 1

Investigate an aspect of the behaviour of magnets

How can you measure the [strength] of a magnet?

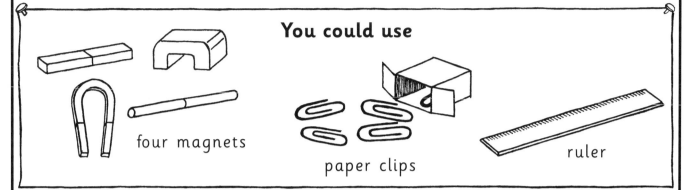

You could use

four magnets

paper clips

ruler

• **Plan a test to find out which is the strongest magnet.**

This is what I shall do:

_____

_____

_____

_____

_____

Draw and write.

I shall keep these things the same:

_____

_____

I shall change only this:

_____

_____

_____

I shall observe and record this:

_____

I shall know which is the strongest magnet because _____

_____

_____

Teachers' note The children should first have completed pages 48–50. Ask them if they can feel any differences between the magnets when they are using them. Which is the strongest? How can they tell? They could predict the order of strength of four magnets and record their prediction by drawing the magnets in order from weakest to strongest. Continued on page 52.

Developing Science
Year 3
© A & C BLACK

Strong magnets: 2

Recognise whether a test is fair or unfair

Are these tests ⎡fair⎤ **?** ⎡Yes⎤ **or** ⎡No⎤

- **Explain your answers.**

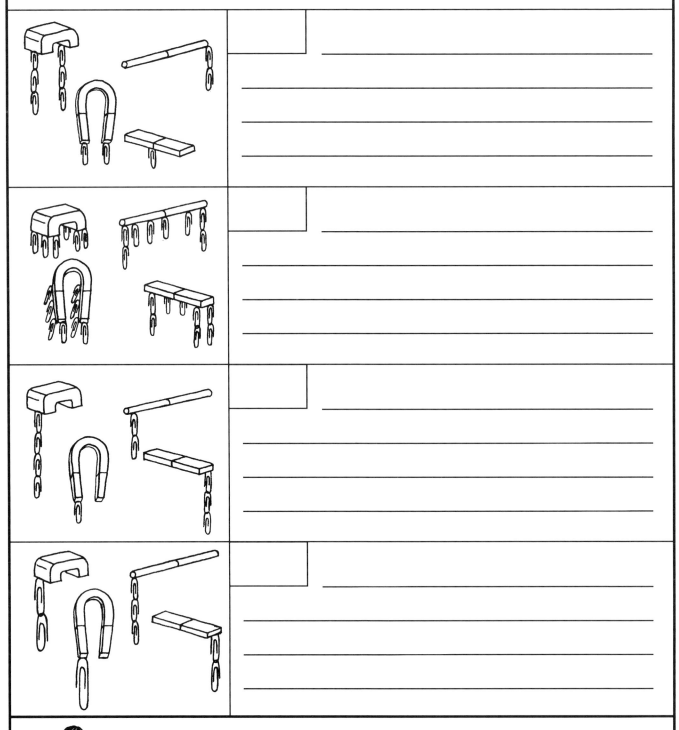

Teachers' note The children should first have completed pages 48–51. Discuss the tests they have planned and, after they have completed this page, ask them to check that their own tests are fair. They could record their results on a simple two-column chart on which they could draw each magnet and then write either how many paper clips it picks up or how far from the magnet the paper clip is attracted.

Developing Science
Year 3
© **A & C BLACK**

Now try this!

What have you found out about the strength of magnets?

52

Pulling through

Investigate an aspect of the behaviour of magnets

Will a magnet work through different materials?

- Find out.

Write on the chart.

paper clip

material being tested

magnet

Material	Prediction	Result
kitchen foil		
cotton fabric		
leather		
steel		
cardboard		
wood		
plastic		
iron		

Now try this!

How can you find out if a magnet works through liquids?

Draw and write about your experiment.

Teachers' note Ask the children if they think a magnet will attract a paper clip through a piece of paper. How do they know? What about other materials? Will a magnet work through all materials? Discuss whether it matters how thick the materials are.

Developing Science Year 3
© A & C BLACK

Springy things

You can find springs **all around you.**

- **Look for springs in the objects you see.**

What are the springs for?

⚠ **Ask permission before taking things apart.**

Object	What the spring is for
torch	
mattress	
ballpoint pen	
clothes peg	

 **Now try this!**

- **Examine something else that has a spring.**
- **Draw and describe the object.**
- **Write about what the spring is for.**

Teachers' note Show the children a jack-in-the-box or another toy featuring a spring, and ask them what the spring does. Encourage them to describe what is happening when they push the spring, why the lid has to be closed to keep the jack-in-the-box in and what happens when they open the lid and why. As a homework activity they could look at home for things that use springs.

Developing Science
Year 3
© **A & C BLACK**

54

Spring into action

Understand that a compressed spring exerts a force

- **Investigate** springs.

You need

a collection of springs

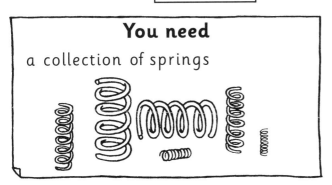

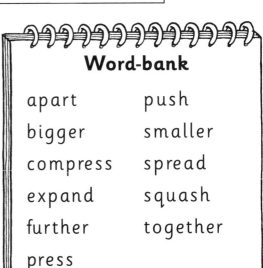

Word-bank

apart	push
bigger	smaller
compress	spread
expand	squash
further	together
press	

- **Draw what happens when you press on a spring.**

- **Draw red arrows to show which way you push.**
  What can you feel?

  _____

  _____

  _____

- **Draw green arrows to show which way the spring pushes.**

What happens when you let go of the spring?

_____

_____

_____

Now try this!

- **Plan a test to find out which is the** strongest **spring.**

Teachers' note Provide some springs for the children to push and ask them to describe what happens. Use the word *force* for 'push' and introduce the word *compress*. Ask the children to point out the direction in which they are pushing and the direction in which the spring is pushing.

Developing Science
Year 3
© A & C BLACK

At a stretch

Understand that a stretched elastic band exerts a force

Mina is stretching an elastic band .

Don't let go suddenly when you stretch an elastic band.

- **Draw red arrows to show which way she is pulling.**

- **Draw green arrows to show which way the elastic band is pulling.**

Mina

- **Describe what happens when you stretch an elastic band.**

_____

_____

_____

_____

_____

Word-bank

expand
longer
pull
push
shorter
spring
stretch
thicker
thinner

- **Describe what happens when you stop stretching it.**

_____

_____

_____

_____

_____

Now try this!

- **Plan an investigation to find out how much an elastic band can stretch.**

Teachers' note Provide some elastic bands for the children to stretch and ask them to describe what happens. Use the word *force* for 'pull'. Ask the children to point out the direction in which they are pulling and the direction in which the elastic band is pulling.

Developing Science
Year 3
© A & C BLACK

Launch pad

Predict the effect of stretching elastic bands by different amounts

You can use ⟦elastic⟧ to make a toy car go:

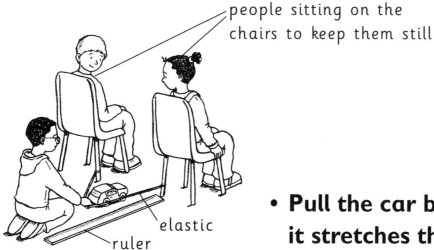

people sitting on the chairs to keep them still

elastic

ruler

• **Pull the car back so that it stretches the elastic.**

• **Record how far the car travels when you pull it back different distances.**

Length of stretch	Distance travelled

Now try this!

If you stretch the elastic more and more, will the car go further and further?

• **Explain your answer to a friend.**

Teachers' note The children should first have completed page 56. Discuss any experience they have of firing or launching objects using elastic bands: for example, catapults and toy aeroplanes. Also discuss the possible dangers and explain that the test they are going to do is safer because it is kept on the ground.

Developing Science
Year 3
© A & C BLACK

Shine a light

- **Stand the cards in a line, as shown in the picture.**

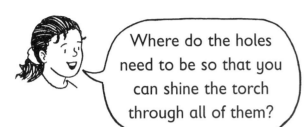

Where do the holes need to be so that you can shine the torch through all of them?

You need

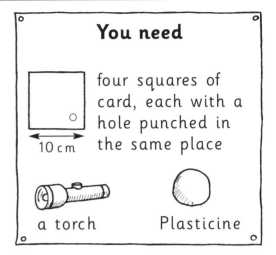

10 cm

four squares of card, each with a hole punched in the same place

a torch   Plasticine

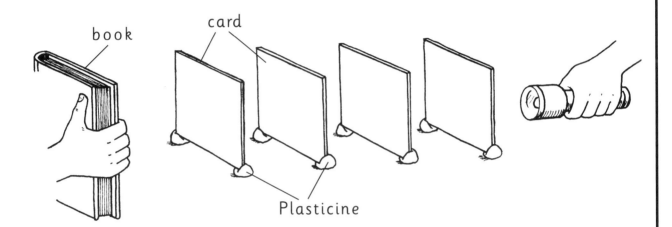

book   card

Plasticine

- **On the picture, draw the holes in the card.**
- **Draw the** light **from the torch.**

  What happens to the beam of light if you turn one of the cards so that the hole is in a different place?

  _____

  _____

Now try this!

- **Write what happens to the beam of light if the book is taken away.**

Teachers' note Before they begin the activity, let the children shine torches through cardboard tubes and through the teeth of a comb. Ask them what they notice about where the light goes. Ask them if it can turn corners. After they have aligned the cards to allow the light to shine through them, ask them to try turning each piece one after the other so that the holes are out of alignment. What do they see on the cards? What shape are the shadows? Why are they this shape?

**Developing Science
Year 3
© A & C BLACK**

Make a shadow

Recognise that shadows are similar in shape to the objects forming them

Investigate shadows .

- **Stand the cocktail stick upright.**

cocktail stick

Plasticine

You need

a cocktail stick

a ball of Plasticine

a torch

- **Make a shadow that is longer than the stick.**

- **Draw and write about what you did.**

_____

_____

_____

_____

What is the longest shadow you can make? _____ c m

- **Make a shadow that is shorter than the stick.**

- **Draw and write about what you did.**

_____

_____

_____

_____

What is the shortest shadow you can make? _____ c m

Now try this!

- **Write instructions for making long and short shadows.**

Teachers' note The children should first have completed page 58. Before they begin this activity ask them to predict the shape of the shadow of the cocktail stick. Ask them to demonstrate how they can change the shape and length of the shadow. After they have completed the activity, ask them if they can suggest any rules for making shadows longer and for making them shorter. Can they make the shadow disappear while shining the torch onto the stick?

Developing Science
Year 3
© A & C BLACK

Compass points

Learn about the points of a compass

- **Look at a** |compass|.
- **Finish the diagram.**

You need

a compass

North

- **Look around your classroom.**
- **On the chart list things you can see in different** |directions|:

North

_____   _____
_____   _____   _____

_____   _____   _____   _____

West   _____   _____   **East**

_____   _____   _____   _____

_____   _____

_____   _____

South

Now try this!

- **List the things you will pass if you walk** |north| **from where you are now.**

Teachers' note Provide the children with accurate compasses (see page 11). Ask them if they know what they are for. Ask them to indicate the direction of north. How can they tell? They might be merely pointing to the direction of 'N' on the compass and not in the direction of its pointer. Point out that north can be in only one direction and that it never changes. Show them how to align 'N' with the pointer. They should all be indicating the same direction now.

Developing Science
Year 3
© **A & C BLACK**

Shadow stick: 1

Understand that shadows change position throughout the day

- **Set up a shadow stick outdoors.**
- **Draw a line to show which way its** shadow **goes.**

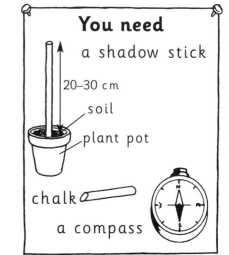

You need

a shadow stick
20–30 cm
soil
plant pot
chalk
a compass

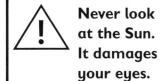
Never look at the Sun. It damages your eyes.

- **Write the time.**
- **Mark the directions:**

| north | south | west | east |

- **Draw the shadow every hour.**
- **At the end of the day draw a diagram to show what happened.**

north
west ——+—— east
south

shadow stick

Now try this!

- **Explain to a friend what happened to the** direction **of the shadow.**

Teachers' note The children should first have completed page 60. Ask them what they noticed about the positions of their own shadows when they went outside at different times on a sunny day. What did they notice when their shadows were in front of them? How could they make their shadows appear behind them? You could ask them to check this before beginning this activity. This activity should be carried out on a sunny day.

Developing Science
Year 3
© A & C BLACK

Shadow stick: 2

- **Measure the** length **of the shadow of your shadow stick.**

- **Record the length of the shadow every hour.**

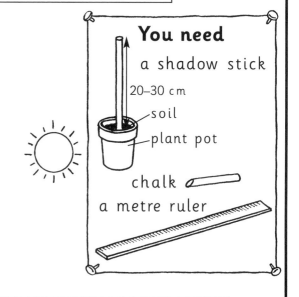

You need

a shadow stick
20–30 cm
soil
plant pot
chalk
a metre ruler

⚠ **Never look at the Sun. It damages your eyes.**

Length of shadow (centimetres)

| 9.00 | 10.00 | 11.00 | 12.00 | 1.00 | 2.00 | 3.00 |

Time

Now try this!

- **Write an explanation of what happened to the length of the shadow.**

Teachers' note The children should first have completed pages 60–61. If they made a life-sized record of the shadows, marked on the ground or on a large piece of paper, the children could check it on another day. If there is a long time interval between the two sets of observations there will be a difference. This time ask them to measure the length of the shadows and colour a column of the graph. Insert a suitable scale. Discuss the pattern shown.

Developing Science Year 3
© A & C BLACK

Shadow clock

Use shadows to tell the time

- **Make a shadow clock.**

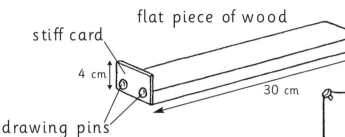

flat piece of wood

stiff card

4 cm

30 cm

drawing pins

⚠ Never look at the Sun. It damages your eyes.

- **Use the shadow clock like this:**

Sun

You need

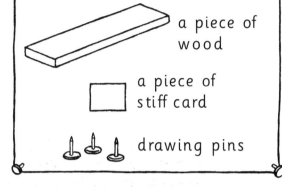

a piece of wood

a piece of stiff card

drawing pins

- **Look at the shadow every hour.**
- **Draw a line.**
- **Write the time.**

- **Draw your finished shadow clock:**

Now try this!

How can you use the shadow clock to tell the time?

- **Write instructions.**

Teachers' note The children should first have completed pages 60–62. To make the shadow clock (which uses the same principle as clocks used in Ancient Egypt) you could substitute a cereal box for the piece of wood. The higher the piece of card used for making the shadow, the longer the base needs to be. Show the children how to point the shadow clock in the direction of the Sun and then to mark the end of the shadow and record the time. The card should always face the Sun.

Developing Science
Year 3
© **A & C BLACK**

Shadow patterns

- **Predict what the** `shadows` **will be like when you shine a torch onto different** `materials` **.**

- **Check your predictions.**

Think about the pattern.

Material	Prediction	Shadow
wood		
net		
wallpaper		
the teeth of a comb		
tissue paper		
voile		

Now try this!

- **Sort a group of materials by the types of shadows they make.**

- **Explain to a friend how you sorted them.**

Teachers' note The children should first have completed pages 58–63. Before they begin this activity it is useful to show them a translucent material such as greaseproof paper and ask them if it will make a shadow. Point out that it lets some light through, so its shadow is not as sharp as that of an object that lets no light through. Introduce or revise the words *opaque, translucent* and *transparent*.

Developing Science
Year 3
© A & C BLACK

Appendix A1

 Private Sector Companies

Agilent Technology (formerly Hewlett Packard):
A division of Hewlett Packard concerned with the design, manufacture and supply of electronic medical equipment.

Barclays Direct Loan Service:
Part of the Barclays Group, employing 644 people and providing phone-a-loan and postal loan service to both Barclays and non-Barclays customers.

BAE SYSTEMS (PROGRAMMES):
Formerly British Aerospace Military Aircraft and Aerostructures, employing over 18,000 people and designing, developing, manufacturing and supporting military aircraft, aircraft structures and associated systems.

BT Payphones:
With a total of 2,038 employees, its business areas are public street payphones, service payphones on privately owned sites and supplying and renting payphones.

DHL International (UK) Limited:
Providing express, door-to-door distribution world-wide, including the overnight delivery of light to medium weight freight and documentation within Europe; employing over 3,500 staff.

NatWest Insurance Services:
A wholly owned subsidiary of National Westminster Bank plc, employing 1,315 staff, and providing general insurance and independent financial advice.

NatWest Mortgage Services:
Provides residential mortgage finance and employs 1,600 staff.

Nortel:
A division of the Canadian company Northern Telecom Limited. Nortel employs 900 people and supplies networked communications solutions to telecommunications service providers.

Post Office Counters:
Employs 12,300 staff. Services include benefit payment, corporate banking, personal banking, savings, insurance, bill payment, bureau de change, mails, telecommunications, lotteries and stationery.

Yellow Pages:
Providing independent advertising, in catalogue and electronic form, for all sectors of business.

Unilever HPC-E:
The European division of Unilever which develops, manufactures and markets products for home and personal care. Brands include Persil, Sure, Lynx, Jif, Organics and Comfort.

 Public Sector Organisations

Civil Service College :
As the largest management school in the country, provides training and development to managers and specialists in government.

Central Office of Communication Publications Group:
An executive agency commissioning print and publishing services, and producing a wide range of publications – annual reports, periodicals, White Papers, leaflets, posters and web sites.

Devon Social Services:
Part of Devon County Council with responsibility for the welfare of the people in Devon, and working with other organisations to provide a range of both counselling and practical services to meet individual needs.

DERA:
A part of the Ministry of Defence responsible for technological developments.

DSS IT Services Agency:
Provides information systems and information technology services to support social security provision.

Employment Services South West:
An Agency within the Department for Education and Employment, helping people to find work and employers to fill their vacancies. It is one of nine regions making up the national Employment Service in Britain.

Foxdenton School and Integrated Nursery:
A state primary school for children aged between 2 and 11, catering primarily for those with special educational needs arising from physical or medical difficulties.

HM Customs and Excise, London Central Collection:
Collection of VAT from employers and traders in the London region.

Humberside Police E Division:
Protects, helps and re-assures the people of Humberside. Reduces crime and the fear of crime in partnership with other agencies.

Inland Revenue Accounts Office, Cumbernauld:
Has responsibility for tax collection, banking and accounting of tax and national insurance contributions.

Inland Revenue NICO Insolvency Group:
An executive agency within the DSS with responsibility for national insurance contributions.

Runshaw College:
A tertiary college providing both A levels and vocational course to adults and school leavers, serving over 20,000 students.

Scottish Homes:
A national housing agency enabling the effective provision of good quality housing and to stimulate self-motivated communities.

Appendix A1 (continued)

 SMEs and Divisional Units

Aeroquip Aerospace Division:
A business employing around 80 people, responsible for designing, manufacturing and supplying fluid handling products to the UK aerospace original equipment manufacturers.

AP Acrefair:
Air Product's European manufacturing facility employing around 285 people and manufacturing key items of cryogenic plant.

Ducker Engineering:
A small business which manufactures, installs and services equipment for the garment sector of the industrial laundry market, producing on-hanger finishing, sorting, folding and transportation systems for the work wear rental sector.

Lawson Mardon Plastics:
The business employs around 150 people and designs and manufactures injection moulded packaging for the food, beverage, cosmetics and healthcare industries.

Seaview Hotel and Restaurant:
An independent owner-managed, small seaside hotel comprising 16 bedrooms, 2 restaurants and 2 bars, with a workforce of 40, serving both the year-round local and tourist trade.

Springfarm Architectural Mouldings Ltd:
A privately owned company employing 54 people, manufacturing a range of architectural mouldings for the construction and DIY industries, which are sold through builders merchants.

Vista Optics Limited:
A privately owned company with 17 employees, manufacturing medical device polymers for intra-ocular and contact lenses.